By Faith Abraham

W M Henry

ISBN: 978-1-78364-463-6

The Open Bible Trust
Fordland Mount, Upper Basildon,
Reading, RG8 8LU, UK.

www.obt.org.uk

By Faith Abraham

Contents

Page

5   Introduction
11   Faith to go out
19   Faith to dwell
25   Faith to become a father
31   God changed his name from Abram to Abraham
32   Gad gave him the covenant of circumcision
32   God changed Sarai's name to Sarah
37   Faith to offer Isaac
47   A Doctrinal Application
55   A Practical Application
64   More on Abraham
70   About the Author
73   Also by W M Henry
75   About this Book

INTRODUCTION

By Faith Abraham   6

INTRODUCTION

The tenth chapter of the epistle to the Hebrews ends with an indirect quotation from the book of Habakkuk:

> "He who is coming will come and will not delay. But my righteous one will live by faith. And if he shrinks back, I will not be pleased with him." (Hebrews 10:37-38).

Paul also quotes Habakkuk in Galatians 3:11 and Romans 1:17. In the former passage the stress is on faith, while in the later, the emphasis is on righteousness or justification, which is possible only through faith. Here in the epistle to the Hebrews, the emphasis is on *living* by faith, that is, persevering in faith to do God's will in the face of opposition. This is not the faith of initial salvation but the mature faith which is defined in Hebrews 11:1:

> "Now faith is being sure of what we hope for and certain of what we do not see."

Following this is a list of those who were not only saved by faith, but who looked forward to what they could not see and who, as a result, persevered in following God's will for them, even though they met opposition, suffering and hardship.

Four times in this list – in verses 8, 9, 11 and 17 – we read of the faith of either Abraham or his wife Sarah, (whose faith was bound up with that of her husband). No Old Testament character is mentioned so many times in the New Testament, where there are over 70 references to Abraham.

He came onto the scene at the end of Genesis 11, and in chapter 12 we read of God promising to bless the world through the seed of Abraham. However, in Hebrews 11, the emphasis is not so much on what God was to do through Abraham as on how Abraham responded to God's promises. It focuses attention on Abraham's own merit and the faith by which this righteous man lived.

In a sense, Abraham's life was a pilgrimage of faith, but Hebrews 11 focuses our attention on 4 separate incidents in his life which mark the growth and strengthening of his trust in the Lord.

FAITH
TO GO OUT

By Faith Abraham   11

FAITH TO GO OUT

"By faith Abraham, when called to go to a place he would later receive as his inheritance, obeyed and went, even though he did not know where he was going." (Hebrews 11:8).

This takes us back to Genesis 12:1, where we read that:

"The Lord had said to Abram, 'Leave your country, your people and your father's household and go to the land I will show you.'"

This command, and the promises that accompanied it, resulted in Abraham moving from Haran into Canaan, but it would appear that the original order to move to Canaan was given earlier, before Abraham and his family arrived in Haran, for, in Genesis 11:31 we read:

"Terah took his son Abram, his grandson Lot, son of Haran, and his daughter-in-law Sarai, the wife of his son Abram, and together they set out from Ur of the Chaldeans to go to Canaan. But when they came to Haran, they settled there."

Here it could appear that Terah was the instigator of the move, but in Acts 7:2-4, Stephen tells us that:

"The God of Glory appeared to our father Abraham while he was still in Mesopotamia, before he lived in Haran. 'Leave your country and your people' God said, 'and go to the land I will show you.'"

So it is more likely that Abraham's call was the reason for the original removal.

At the time God called him, Abraham was living in Ur among a family of idolators, (see Joshua 24:2). In order to be free to follow the Lord properly, he would have to separate himself from them, hence the Lord's command to leave his family. But Abraham took both Terah and Lot with him. Though the destination should have been Canaan, they stopped and settled in Haran. The reason for the delay is not given but Terah was most likely the cause, because God's renewed command to Abraham came only after his father's death, as Stephen points out:

"After the death of his father, God sent him to this land where you are now living." (Acts 7:4)

So Abraham went into the land, but he still had Lot with him, and the Lord did not speak with him in detail until he had separated from Lot:

"The Lord said to Abram after Lot had parted from him, 'Lift up your eyes from where you are and look north and south, east and west. All the land that you see I will give to you and your offspring for ever.'" (Genesis 13:14-15).

As a result of these hindrances, and Abraham's reluctance to obey immediately, he was more than 75 years old (Genesis 12:4) before he was in a position to receive God's full blessing. Yet, in spite of the delays, Abraham was counted faithful because he did obey. His faith manifested itself in action, and although the action was hesitant at first, in time he came to the land he had been promised those many years before.

In considering Abraham's obedience it is important to realise the major step of faith he was taking. Hebrews 11:8 tells us that he went out "even though he did not know where he was going." God had promised Abraham that he would reach a land "I will show you" (Genesis 12:1). He had seen nothing of this land in advance, but, believing the One who had made the promise, he went out.

In addition, we have to remember what he was leaving behind. Excavations in Ur of the Chaldeans have revealed that it was no primitive settlement, but was a substantial city with a considerable culture. Abraham was not a wandering tribesman and the ties with city life must have been difficult to break. Certainly, Terah found it impossible and went no further than

Haran. Even in the land of Canaan, Lot, after leaving Abraham, became a city dweller again, in Sodom, with nearly disastrous consequences.

However, Abraham was prepared to renounce these comforts and become a tent dweller, to follow the call of the Lord wherever it might lead him, even though the Lord was a God whom his fathers did not know.

FAITH
TO DWELL

FAITH TO DWELL

"By faith he made his home in the promised land like a stranger in a foreign country; he lived in tents, as did Isaac and Jacob, who were heirs with him of the same promise." (Hebrews 11:9).

The testing of Abraham's faith was not over when he reached the promised land. He had been told that the land would be given to him and his offspring. When the Lord appeared to Abraham at Shechem, He told him: "To your offspring I will give this land." (Genesis 12:7). This was repeated in more detail after Lot had departed:

> "The Lord said to Abram after Lot had parted from him …All the land that you see I will give to you and your offspring for ever… Go, walk through the length and breadth of the land, for I am giving it to you." (Genesis 13:14-17).

Later, this land is defined as being from "the river of Egypt to the great river, the Euphrates." (Genesis 15:18).

However, it was not simply a question of walking into the land and taking possession of it. During his lifetime Abraham never owned all this land, living permanently in his tent. He depended on the Lord to fulfil His promises in His own good time. This attitude of dependence on the Lord alone is illustrated by his dealings with the king of Sodom. Following his daring rescue of Lot and the other captives from Kedorlaomer, Abraham rebuffed the king's offer of the spoils with the words:

> "I have raised my hand to the Lord, God most High, Creator of heaven and earth, and have taken an oath that I will accept nothing belonging to you not even a thread or the thong of a sandal, so that you will never be able to say 'I made Abram rich.'" (Genesis 14:22, 23).

Abraham, who had been promised so much by God, did not want God's glory given to another when these promises were fulfilled So he was content to remain a stranger in the land that had been promised to him and his descendents.

But Hebrews 11 tells us more than the Genesis account. In verse 10 we are told why he was content to remain a nomad:

"For he was looking forward to the city with foundations, whose architect and builder is God."

Abraham was content, for he was looking beyond the land itself to the heavenly city the heavenly Jerusalem of Hebrews 12:22 which is described in more detail in Revelation 21.

The attitude of Abraham, Isaac and Jacob and the other giants of faith is summed up in Hebrews 11:13-16:

"All these people were still living by faith when they died. They did not receive the things promised; they only saw them and welcomed them from a distance… they were longing for a better country – a heavenly one. Therefore God is not ashamed to be called their God, for he has prepared a city for them."

FAITH
TO BECOME A
FATHER

By Faith Abraham 25

FAITH TO BECOME A FATHER

"By faith Abraham, even though he was past age – and Sarah herself was barren – was enabled to become a father because he considered him faithful who had made the promise." (Hebrews 11:11).

There is an ambiguity in the text here and the New International Version gives as an alternative:

"By faith even Sarah, who was past age, was enabled to bear children because she considered him faithful who had made the promise."

So there is doubt as to whether the faith was Abraham's or Sarah's. As we examine the Old Testament account of the events leading up to the birth of Isaac, however, we find that the faith spoken of here was primarily Abraham's. When he arrived in Canaan, Abraham had been promised

"To your offspring I will give this land." (Genesis 12:7). But Abraham and Sarah had no children and as they grew older, the chances of a child diminished and eventually disappeared. Abraham was obviously perplexed by this and, when, following his encounter with the king of Sodom, God spoke to him promising him a very great reward, Abraham came straight to the point:

"'O Sovereign Lord, what can you give me since I remain childless and the one who will inherit my estate is Eliezer of Damascus?' And Abram said, 'You have given me no children; so a servant in my household will be my heir.' Then the word of the Lord came to him: 'This man will not be your heir, but a son coming from your own body will be your heir.' He took him outside and said, 'Look up at the heavens and count the stars – if indeed you can count them.' Then he said to him, 'So shall your offspring be.' Abram believed the Lord and he credited it to him as righteousness." (Genesis 15:2-6).

The climax of this narrative is so brief, but so important. Abraham's belief in the word of the Lord against all his natural instincts was such that the Lord counted it as righteousness. This incident is taken up by Paul in the epistle to the Romans and used to show that the basis of Abraham's salvation was not works, but faith:

"What then shall we say that Abraham, our forefather, discovered in this matter? If, in fact, Abraham was justified by works, he had something to boast about – but not before God. What does the Scripture say? 'Abraham believed God, and it was credited to him as righteousness.'" (Romans 4:1-3).

Paul was at pains to emphasise Abraham's faith in the matter.

"Against all hope, Abraham in hope believed and so became the father of many nations, just as it had been said to him, 'So shall your offspring be.' Without weakening in his faith, he faced the fact that his body was as good as dead – since he was about a hundred years old

– and that Sarah's womb was also dead. Yet he did not waver through unbelief regarding the promise of God, but was strengthened in his faith and gave glory to God, being fully persuaded that God had power to do what he had promised. This is why 'it was credited to him as righteousness'" (Romans 4:18-22).

Abraham believed God – the God who gives life to the dead (Romans 4:17) but his faith was not rewarded immediately. He spent 10 years in the land of Canaan (Genesis 16:3) with no prospects of a son. By this time Sarah was determined that they should take matters into their own hands:

"Now Sarai, Abram's wife, had borne him no children. But she had an Egyptian maidservant named Hagar; so she said to Abram, 'The Lord has kept me from having children. Go, sleep with my maidservant; perhaps I can build a family through her.'" (Genesis 16:1-2).

This was legal in that society and the child would be counted as Abraham and Sara's son, so

Abraham agreed to this plan and Ishmael was born when Abraham was 86. (Genesis 16:16). However, was God intending to fulfil His promise in Ishmael?

Thirteen more years were to pass before God again spoke to Abraham, and at that point He confirmed the permanence of His dealings with him in three ways:

1. God changed his name from Abram (exalted father) to Abraham (father of many).

"When Abram was ninety-nine years old, the Lord appeared to him and said, 'I am God Almighty; walk before me and be blameless. I will confirm my covenant between me and you will greatly increase your numbers... No longer will you be called Abram; your name will be Abraham, for I have made you a father of many nations. I will make you very fruitful; I will make nations of you, and kings will come from you... The whole land of Canaan, where you are now an alien, I will give as an everlasting possession to you and your descendants after you; and I will be their God.'" (Genesis 17:1-8).

2. God gave him the covenant of circumcision.

"This is my covenant with you and your descendants after you, the covenant you are to keep: Every male among you shall be circumcised. You are to undergo circumcision, and it will be the sign of the covenant between me and you. For the generations to come every male among you who is eight days old must be circumcised…Any uncircumcised male… will be cut off from his people." (Genesis 17:10-14).

3. God changed Sarai's name (barren) to Sarah (princess).

"As for Sarai your wife, you are no longer to call her Sarai; her name will be Sarah…

I will bless her so that she will be the mother of nations; kings of peoples will come from her." (Genesis 17:15-16).

Abraham's immediate reaction was amazement. He had apparently regarded Ishmael as the fulfilment of the Lord's promise, for he said to God, "If only Ishmael might live under your blessing" (Genesis 17:18). God's reply was unequivocal:

> "Yes, but your wife Sarah will bear you a son, and you will call him Isaac. I will establish my covenant with him as an everlasting covenant for his descendants after him… My covenant I will establish with Isaac, whom Sarah will bear to you by this time next year." (Genesis 17:19, 21).

And Abraham's response to all this was immediate obedience.

> "On that very day Abraham took his son Ishmael and all those born in his household or bought with his money, every male in his

household, and circumcised them, as God told him." (Genesis 17:23).

Even though the situation seemed impossible, for Sarah was past child-bearing age, Abraham's faith in the One Who had promised was unwavering.

The time was now approaching for Isaac to be born. The Lord reconfirmed His promise once more – when He appeared to Abraham in the plains of Mamre, prior to the destruction of Sodom. He said:

"I will surely return to you about this time next year, and Sarah your wife will have a son." (Genesis 18:10).

Sarah's reaction was to laugh in the privacy of her tent, but she was shocked when the Lord asked Abraham:

"Why did Sarah laugh and say, 'Will I really have a child now that I am old?' Is anything too hard for the Lord?" (verses 13-14).

We are not told of Abraham's response, but at the appointed time Isaac was born.

Sarah was filled with joy and pride. She declared:

> "God has brought me laughter, and everyone who hears about this will laugh with me... Who would have said to Abraham that Sarah would nurse children? Yet I have borne him a son in his old age." (Genesis 21:6-7).

Isaac had completely taken over any place Ishmael may have held in her affections. When Ishmael mocked Isaac, she would not allow it:

> "Get rid of that slave woman and her son, for that slave woman's son will never share in the inheritance with my son Isaac." (Genesis 21:10).

So the little family was complete. Abraham's faith had been rewarded and the son through whom all God's promises would be fulfilled had come. But the greatest trial of Abraham's faith was still ahead.

FAITH TO OFFER ISAAC

FAITH TO OFFER ISAAC

"By faith Abraham, when God tested him, offered Isaac as a sacrifice. He who had received the promises was about to sacrifice his one and only son, even though God had said to him, 'It is through Isaac that your offspring will be reckoned'" (Hebrews 11:17-18).

Consider the circumstances; Abraham and Sarah, having waited so long for a son of promise, had been rewarded in their old age. The boy was growing up in the care of his proud parents, when the word of the Lord came to Abraham.

"Take your son, your only son Isaac, whom you love, and go to the region of Moriah. Sacrifice him there as a burnt offering on one of the mountains I will tell you about." (Genesis 22:2).

God did not spare Abraham's feelings in this matter. He emphasised – "your *son*… your *only* son… whom you *love*." He showed Abraham that He was aware of what such a course of action would mean to him. The prospect must have been appalling. Yet what was Abraham's reaction?

> "Early the next morning Abraham got up and saddled his donkey. He took with him two of his servants and his son Isaac. When he had cut enough wood for the burnt offering, he set out for the place God had told him about." (Genesis 22:3).

Abraham had more than two days (Genesis 22:4) to think of what he was about to do. Unable to confide in Sarah, Isaac or his servants, he was alone with his thoughts. Yet there is no record of him hesitating or complaining. He new that God's promises must be fulfilled through Isaac, even though this latest instruction seemed to negate all possibility of this. Yet Abraham continued to believe these promises would be fulfilled. What was the secret of his belief? The explanation is given in Hebrews 11:19.

"Abraham reasoned that God could raise the dead, and figuratively speaking, he did receive Isaac back from death."

Abraham knew that he was dealing with a God who could produce life from death. He had already seen God's power in this direction demonstrated in his own body, and that of Sarah's. Isaac was born because Abraham had faced his own deadness without faltering in his faith.

"Without weakening in his faith, he faced the fact that his body was as good as dead – since he was about a hundred years old – and that Sarah's womb was also dead. Yet he did not waver through unbelief regarding the promise of God, but was strengthened in his faith and gave glory to God, being fully persuaded that God had power to do what He had promised." (Romans 4:19-21).

Similarly, in this new situation, Abraham reasoned that God could bring Isaac back to life, and that He would do so, to fulfil His promises. In a sense, that is what happened.

The unwavering nature of Abraham's faith is clearly seen in the Genesis account of events. As he left his servants he gave them instructions:

"Stay here with the donkey while I and the boy go over there. We will worship and then we will come back to you." (Genesis 22:5).

Abraham did not anticipate returning to his servants alone. He had no doubt in his mind that Isaac would live, even though he might have to be sacrificed first. In response to Isaac's puzzled question concerning the lamb, he replied: "God himself will provide the lamb for the burnt offering, my son," (Genesis 22:8) – a prophetic statement since God did, in fact, provide a ram for the sacrifice. But Abraham obeyed the Lord's instructions fully. Verse 10 of the chapter makes it clear that he was at the very point of sacrificing his son before the angel of the Lord stopped him.

As we read this episode we may wonder at the apparently unnecessary torment to which Abraham was subjected. Yet we should remember that some 2000 years later there was to be another

Son, an only Son, a Son loved by His Father, Who was sacrificed. And in His case, there was no ram substituted.

Abraham, the father, and Isaac the only son, are types of *the* Father and *the* Son and by visualising what Abraham must have suffered on his journey to sacrifice Isaac, we may have a glimpse of something of the cost to the Father in sending His only beloved Son to the cross.

The Lord Jesus Christ went to the Cross and there paid the penalty for our sin, achieving what no rams, goats or bulls could ever achieve – an effectual atonement for sin.

"It is impossible for the blood of bulls and goats to take away sins…"BUT" …we have been made holy through the sacrifice of the body of Jesus Christ once for all. Day after day every priest stands and performs his religious duties; again and again he offers the same sacrifices, which can never take away sins. But when this priest had offered for all time one sacrifice for sins, he sat down at the right hand of God." (Hebrews 10:4, 10-12).

God, seeing what was ahead, was sharing in the agony of mind that Abraham suffered, but to a much greater extent. He intended that Isaac would be delivered. There was to be no deliverance for the Lord Jesus.

What was the reason for this incident? Genesis 22:1 states that God was testing Abraham, and, after Abraham had come through the test, the Lord's conclusion recorded in verses 16-18 was:

> "Because you have done this and have not withheld your son, your only son, I will surely bless you and make your descendants as numerous as the stars in the sky and as the sand on the seashore. Your descendants will take possession of the cities of their enemies, and through your offspring all nations on earth will be blessed, because you have obeyed me."

Abraham had been called to go out from Ur, leaving his family. He went, but took his father and nephew with him. He was told to go into the promised land of Canaan but he lingered in Haran until his father was dead. He was promised a son, but he did not wait for the Lord to fulfil His promise through Sarah. Abraham believed God but his faith, great though it was, was not complete. The Lord's instruction after the birth of Ishmael was "walk before me and be blameless." (Genesis 17:1).

Abraham's faith was growing all the time and it seems that, with the birth of Isaac, his faith matured – no more would he obey partially; no more would he leave Canaan for Egypt when famine threatened; no more would he lie to Abimelech or Pharaoh to protect himself. His trust in God was total and when the greatest test of all came, his faith stood firm.

A
DOCTRINAL
APPLICATION

A DOCTRINAL APPLICATION

In Romans 4, as we have seen, Paul explains that Abraham's faith in God's promise of a son was such that "it was credited to him as righteousness." But he goes on to point out that these facts were recorded not only for Abraham's benefit.

> "The words, 'it was credited to him' were written not for him alone, but *also for us, to whom God will credit righteousness* – for us who believe in him who raised Jesus our Lord from the dead. He was delivered over to death for our sins and was raised to life for our justification." (Romans 4:23-25).

Throughout this chapter, Paul has been using Abraham as an illustration of the great doctrinal truth that he has expounded in chapter 3 – namely that a righteousness from God was being made known. This was quite different from any righteousness which could be attained by law-keeping, but it was no new concept. The law and the Prophets had testified to it. This righteousness was extended by God to *all* who believe, through faith in Christ Jesus, whether they were circumcised or uncircumcised (Romans 3:22).

Man's problem is that his situation before God is hopeless. Having considered both Jew and Gentile (Romans 3:9-10), Paul's conclusion on the matter is:

"No-one will be declared righteous in his (God's) sight by observing the law; rather, through the law we become conscious of sin." (Romans 3:20).

He is not referring only to the law of Moses. He is saying something much more fundamental – that by keeping rules (no matter what they are) no one can be declared righteous in the sight of God. In fact, laws have a different effect – they identify sin and point it out to the person involved, proving to him that he is a sinner. This gives us a clue as to a major function of the law. It was not designed to give man rules to obey, in order to earn his salvation. Instead it was given to show him his own weakness, sinfulness and his need of a Saviour.

"The law was put in charge to lead us to Christ that we might be justified by faith." (Galatians 3:24).

So, Paul says, as far as sin is concerned, there is no difference between Jew and Gentile before God:

"for *all* have sinned and fall short of the glory of God, and are justified freely by his grace through the redemption that came by Christ Jesus." (Romans 3:23-24).

The Lord Jesus was offered as a sacrifice for sins – the true reality behind many of the Old Testament pictures of sacrifice – including Abraham's offering of Isaac. Why was such an extreme measure as death on a cross necessary? Paul explains:

"God presented him as a sacrifice of atonement, through faith in his blood… He did it to demonstrate his justice at the present time, so as to be just and the one who justifies the man who has faith in Jesus." (Romans 3:25-26).

God was showing that the reason he had overlooked men's sin in the past was not that He was unrighteous. On the contrary, God is both just and righteous. Men are sinners and all are utterly condemned before Him. In order for them to be accepted by Him, it would have been necessary for God to ignore their sin, but because of His righteousness He could not do this. So there would appear to be no hope for mankind unless the penalty for sin could somehow be paid.

This is what God accomplished for us through Christ. His love for us was so great that He sent the Lord Jesus Christ into the world, to pay the penalty for our sin in order that He could justify us and at the same time remain just Himself. Sin was therefore not overlooked. The wages of sin is death and this price was paid when Christ died.

God's just requirements have been met through the work of Christ and the sinner can be offered forgiveness and justification through that same work on the cross. This was God's plan all along. Justification could never come about by obedience to law, and Abraham is a classic illustration of salvation by faith. Abraham was not without merit. He was a man of bravery and devotion to his family – as is apparent from his rescue of Lot. But the Scripture says:

"Abraham believed God, and it was credited to him as righteousness." (Romans 4:3).

Abraham was a good man. But he was justified not by his works but by his faith – faith in the power of God "who gives life to the dead, and calls things that are not as though they were." (Romans 4:17). In the same way, righteousness is credited to us, not on the basis of our works, but on the basis of our faith in the One who raised the Lord Jesus Christ from the dead "for our justification." (Romans 4:25).

A PRACTICAL APPLICATION

A PRACTICAL APPLICATION

Having considered the great list of faithful servants of God including Abraham, in Hebrews 11, we are now given encouragement for our daily lives from the example of these great men.

> "Therefore, since we are surrounded by such a great cloud of witnesses, let us throw off everything that hinders and the sin that so easily entangles, and let us run with perseverance the race marked out for us." (Hebrews 12:1).

Abraham had been promised a land, yet he never inherited it in his lifetime. He had been promised descendants "as numerous as the stars in the sky and as countless as the sand on the seashore," yet ye had to wait so long before Isaac was born. Abraham and the other "witnesses" are characterised by their perseverance in difficult situations, and chapter 11 finishes with the words:

"These were all commended for their faith, yet none of them received what had been promised. God had planned something better for us so that only together with us would they be made perfect." (Hebrews 11:39-40).

Abraham's eyes were fixed on the "city with foundations, whose architect and builder is God", (Hebrews 11:10), and because of this he was able to cope with his trials and problems.

In the same way, we must continue steadfast, not setting our affection on achieving fulfilment from the things of this life. This exhortation to persevere is a resumption of the theme of chapter 10 where we read:

"Let us hold unswervingly to the hope we profess, for he who promised is faithful. And let us consider how we may spur one another on towards love and good deeds." (Hebrews 10:32-36).

Following their conversion, these Hebrew believers had stood up well to difficulties, and they were encouraged not to forget this:

"Remember those earlier days after you had received the light, when you stood your ground in a great contest in the face of suffering. Sometimes you were publicly exposed to insult and persecution; at other times you stood side by side with those who were so treated. You sympathised with those in prison and joyfully accepted the confiscation of your property, because you knew that you yourselves had better and lasting possessions. So do not throw away your confidence; it will be richly rewarded. You need to persevere so that when you have done the will of God you will receive what he has promised." (Hebrews 10:32-36).

The secret of these believers' early success and their hopes of future success lay in turning their eyes away from their present plight and fixing their gaze on God and His promises. This was what Abraham had done and the Hebrews were urged to fix their eyes on the greatest example of all – the Lord Jesus Christ.

> "Let us fix our eyes on Jesus, the author and perfector of our faith, who for the joy set before him endured the cross, scorning its shame, and sat down at the right hand of the throne of God. Consider him who endured such opposition from sinful men, so that you will not grow weary and lose heart." (Hebrews 12:2-3).

The Lord Jesus Christ, the pioneer and perfector of our faith, endured the cross and all that went with it for the joy set before Him. Abraham endured the hardships of a nomadic existence for the joy set before *him*, and the command to us is to follow in their footsteps.

Living in the world, believers are bound to suffer persecution and hardship. They are not at home here. When the Lord prayed to His Father in John 17, He set out their position very clearly:

"I have given them (His disciples) your word and the world has hated them, for they are not of the world any more that I am of the world. My prayer is not that you take them out of the world but that you protect them from the evil one. They are not of the world, even as I am not of it." (John 17:14-16).

In fact, Paul echoed these sentiments to Timothy declaring that "everyone who wants to live a godly life in Christ Jesus will be persecuted." (2 Timothy 3:12). Such opposition is only to be expected. We must be prepared to face it, and endure it. Abraham is an example set before us to encourage us. Abraham fixed his eyes on the promise made to him and so should we.

The promise to us, expressed in a "trustworthy saying" is:

"If we died with him, we will also live with him; if we endure we will also reign with him." (2 Timothy 2:11).

But there is also a twofold consolation for us during our lives on earth, and this is set out for us in Hebrews 12.

1. No matter how much persecution we receive, we know that none of us can suffer to the same extent as the Lord, who not only endured the physical pain and humiliation of death on a cross, but who actually became sin for us "so that in him we might become the righteousness of God." (2 Corinthians 5:21). The Hebrew believers had not yet been called upon to be martyrs: -

   "In your struggle against sin, you have not yet resisted to the point of shedding your blood." (Hebrews 12:4).

2. The suffering that we endure is regarded by the Lord as discipline for His sons, and is therefore given us, not to break us, but to strengthen us.

   "You have forgotten that word of encouragement that addresses you as sons: 'My son, do not make light of the Lord's discipline, and do not lose heart when he rebukes you, because the Lord disciplines those whom he loves, and he punishes everyone he accepts as a son.' Endure hardship as a discipline; God is treating you as sons… No discipline seems pleasant at the time, but painful. Later on, however, it produces a harvest of righteousness and peace for those who have been trained by it." (Hebrews 12:5-7, 11).

In order to "live godly in Christ Jesus," we must look beyond the problems and opposition, to the Lord and His promises for us. This was the secret to the maturing of Abraham's faith, and the Lord will achieve the same in us, if we will follow the example of Abraham in perseverance.

MORE ABOUT ABRAHAM

Abraham and his seed
By William Henry, Michael Penny and Sylvia Penny

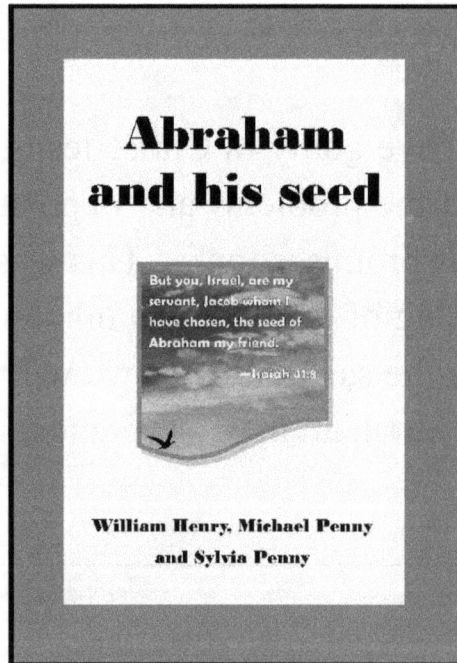

In Genesis 12, we read of God's covenant promise to Abraham to make him a great nation, to bless him and to bless all people on earth through him. As we progress through Genesis, this covenant was confirmed with Abraham and with his immediate seed, Isaac and Jacob. Later, further promises were made to his subsequent seed, the Twelve Tribes of Israel.

How were these promises to be implemented as the seed of Abraham grew into a nation - a nation that largely failed to follow the Lord faithfully as their father Abraham had done? What does the rest of the Old Testament have to say about the seed of Abraham? Was there any change in the New Testament? Where do those who are not the physical seed of Abraham (i.e. Gentiles) fit into all this?

This book traces the Lord's dealings with Abraham and his seed throughout the Old and New Testaments and considers whether God is still dealing with the seed of Abraham today.

Abraham
By James Poole

The author takes the reader through the life of Abraham. Starting with the call by God, James Poole follows Abraham from Ur of the Chaldees, to Haran, into the Promised Land, onto Egypt and then back to Canaan.

Abraham

James Poole

But as well as the geographic journey he also put before the readers the journey of Abraham faith; his justifying faith when he believed God who then considered Abraham righteous. However, as we continue with Abraham we see lapses in his trust of God, but in the end we find a man who has such faith in God that he was willing to sacrifice Isaac, his only son, because he was so convinced that God would have to raise Isaac from the dead if God was to keep his promises.

Abraham's Progress in the Covenants of God

By Glen Burch

This publication commences with an explanation of covenants in general, before turning to the specific covenants that God made with Abraham, which are dealt with and covered well. However, the main theme is Abraham's progress in those covenants.

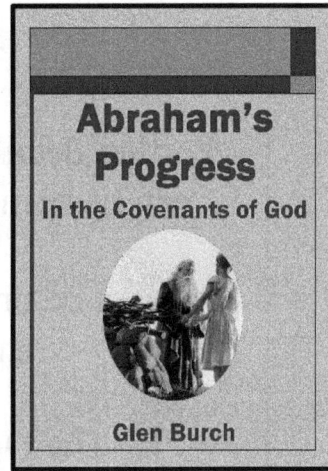

In the preface the author introduces Abraham's life as a pattern that can help Christian's today, and this theme is developed and continues throughout the booklet. In Abraham, then, we find an example of faith that should attract and motivate every Christian.

This booklet will be a blessing to all Christians, especially those who are new to the faith or new to reading the Bible.

Please note:

Further details of all the books here can be seen on **www.obt.org.uk**

The can be ordered from the website and also from

The Open Bible Trust,
Fordland Mount, Upper Basildon,
Reading, RG8 8LU, UK.

They are also available as eBooks from Amazon and Apple,
and also as KDP paperbacks from Amazon.

Portraits of the Patriarchs

By William Henry, Andrew Marple, Michael Penny and Sylvia Penny

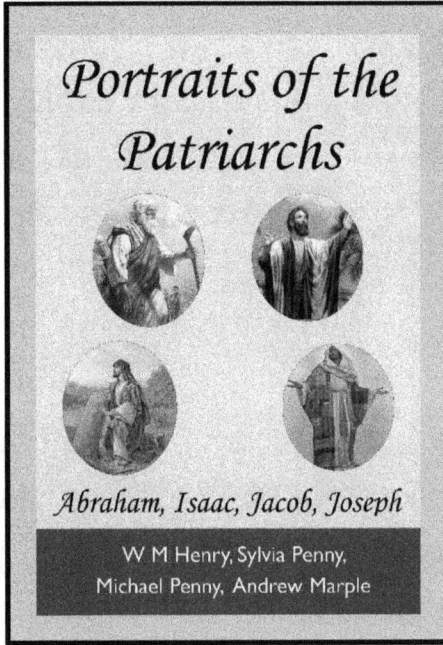

Portraits of the Patriarchs is based on Abraham, Isaac, Jacob and Joseph.

The four authors do an excellent job of not only bringing before us the important issues in the lives of the four patriarchs (i.e. lessons in history). They also, in considering the lives and experiences of Abraham, Isaac, Jacob and Joseph, draw out lessons of faith and practice which are applicable to 21st century Christians.

ABOUT THE AUTHOR

W. M. Henry was born in Glasgow in 1949. He qualified as a Chartered Accountant and worked in the accountancy profession for a number of years before moving into academia. He is now retired and lives in Giffnock with his wife and two daughters. He is an international speaker and has spoken in Canada, Australia and the Netherlands. He has recently had published a major book, *The Trinity in John*: see later for details.

Other publications by W M Henry include:

The Signs in John's Gospel
Covenants: Old and New
No Condemnation – Romans 5:12-8:39
Living in the Truth
That you may know – 1 John
The Speeches in Acts ..... By Faith Abraham
The Making of a Man of God ..... Imitating Christ

W M Henry has also written a number of books
with Michael Penny including:

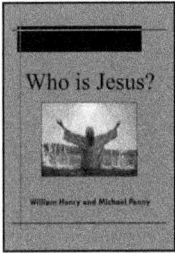

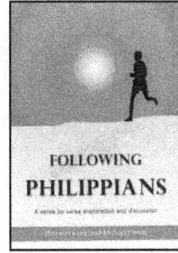

Who is Jesus?
A study based on Matthew 16:13-16

The Will of God: Past and Present.
In the Bible and in the 21st Century

Sit! Walk! Stand!
The Christian life in Ephesians

Following Philippians
A verse by verse exploration and discussion

Further details of these can be seen on
www.obt.org.uk
And they can be ordered from that website

W M Henry is a frequent contributor to *Search* magazine

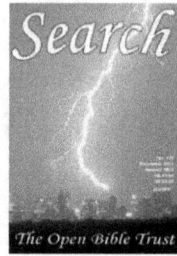

ALSO BY
W M HENRY

The Trinity in John
A study in relationships

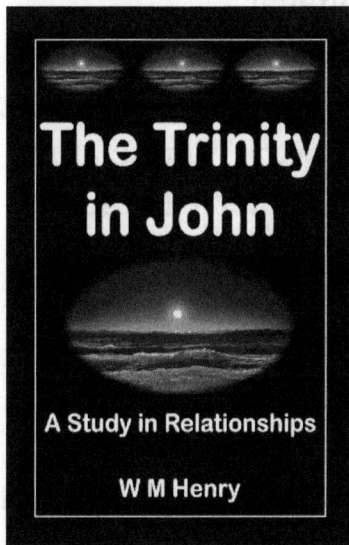

This book is a study of the relationships between the members of the Trinity and between the Trinity and Christian believers, focusing mainly on the Gospel of John.

It opens with a discussion of the titles given to the Lord Jesus in John's Gospel and what they tell us about His relationship with His Father.

Section two explores the relationship between the Father and the Son and their joint work of redemption.

The book then widens the focus to examine the relationship between the Father, the Son and the believer before discussing the Holy Spirit and His relationship with other members of the Trinity, and with the believer.

Each chapter closes with brief meditative "Reflections" on the implications of the issues raised in the chapter. These are followed by suggestions for further study, which can be the basis for private devotions or group discussions.

****

All the publications mentioned in this book can be ordered from **www.obt.org.uk** or from

The Open Bible Trust, Fordland Mount, Upper Basildon, Reading, RG8 8LU, UK.

They are also available as eBooks from Amazon and Apple and as KDP paperbacks from Amazon

****

By Faith Abraham   74

ABOUT THIS BOOK

By Faith Abraham

Hebrews chapter 11 records that:

- By faith Abraham when called went, even though he did not know where he was going!
- By faith Abraham made his home in the Promised Land like a stranger!
- By faith Abraham, even though he was past age, became a father!
- By faith Abraham, when tested, offered up Isaac.

William Henry considers each of these with references back to Genesis, giving much helpful background. He concludes the booklet with doctrinal and practical applications which are pertinent and relevant to all who have faith today.

www.ingramcontent.com/pod-product-compliance
Lightning Source LLC
Chambersburg PA
CBHW060658030426
42337CB00017B/2680